S0-ADY-884

THE STORY

PERRY DUGGAR

WITH A STUDY GUIDE BY **ALLEN WHITE**

HE CAME • HE DIED • HE AROSE
HE ASCENDED • HE'S COMING BACK

THE STORY©

The Story, including the *Small Group Study Guide*, published as a special edition for Brookwood Church

Published by Brookwood Resources
580 Brookwood Point Place
Simpsonville, SC 29681

Small Group Study Guide by Allen White
How to Receive Christ from Study Guide by Ned Gable
Cover design by Lonnie Gilbert
Interior design and layout by Chris Parker and Chip Acker

Printed by Hayne Collins, Printing on the Side, Graycourt, SC
Printed in association with Primus Source, LLC, Taylors, SC

ISBN 978-1-933660-66-0 (Hardback with Study Guide)

Dedication

I want to dedicate this book to three women who have filled my life with beauty.

> *The man who finds a wife finds a treasure, and he receives favor from the Lord.*
>
> – Proverbs 18:22 (NLT)

God has indeed favored me. I truly found a treasure in my lovely wife Leigh Ann. She has faithfully encouraged, supported, and at times, confronted me, but always loved me for over twenty years. In that time, I have caught many wonderful glimpses of what it means to experience an intimate relationship with another person the way a Christian can with Jesus. (Ephesians 5:31-32)

> *Children are a blessing and a gift from the LORD.*
>
> – Psalm 127:3 (CEV)

God has blessed me with two precious gifts in my teenaged daughters, Evan (age 19) and Aubrey (age 17). These delightful young women have enriched my life in immeasurable and innumerable ways. When I reflect on my depth of love for them, I discern in small measure how much God loves His children.

Table of Contents

The Story by Perry Duggar

Small Group Study Guide by Allen White

Appreciation

I want to express a special word of appreciation to Barbara West who provided insightful suggestions, consistent encouragement, and thorough, careful editing of my manuscript. I also want to thank Mark Bagwell, Allen White and Steve Wolverton for reading the manuscript and providing helpful comments. Chip Acker and Lonnie Gilbert aided with the look, feel and flow of the book. I am deeply indebted to these people for their interest and valuable contributions to this project.

Forward

I met for lunch with Peter Sullivan, a friend and businessman, who asked whether I had an interest in writing. I responded immediately that I did, but had never written anything for publication. He told me about his idea for a book. Peter showed me several items his company produced which displayed five symbols. These symbols appeared to be hand-drawn, and provided a clear and compelling visual for explaining the story of Jesus. Peter said the symbols appeared on t-shirts, hats, mugs, plaques, bracelets, bumper stickers, and even tattoos. These items had been distributed throughout the country and beyond. He related that many people were coming to faith through the use of this simple graphic. Peter asked me to write a book to explain the meaning of these symbols. I was greatly honored and very interested!

Writing this book has been an enjoyable experience. My goal has been to summarize the essential elements of Jesus' life, explaining what the Bible says about the extraordinary life of our Savior. I sought to present deep spiritual truths in a simple, understandable way. I avoided injecting personal opinions or imposing a particular interpretive "grid" over the information. I provided supplemental materials dealing with matters which someone new to Jesus' story might find confusing. My purpose is to present clear, simple explanations of deep, complex, theological themes. I also want to broaden thinking in areas where Christians who embrace the Bible often disagree.

My hope is that this book will be an instrument to lead people into an intimate relationship with God through His Son. My prayer is that harmony among believers regarding the essentials of our faith will be encouraged. We know that being united in the body of Christ is of great importance. It is how the world will know we are Jesus' disciples.

> *"Your love for another will prove to the world that you are my disciples."*
>
> – John 13:35 (NLT)

Introduction

We all love stories… stories that surprise us and leave us filled with wonder. Good stories hold our attention. They interest and entertain us. They might teach a truth or provide a lesson. They captivate our minds and affect our emotions. But truly great stories can also shape our lives.

The story of Jesus will amaze and astonish. It will teach and inspire. But most of all, it will change us if we allow it. Jesus' story shows us the way to reach God. Jesus said of Himself,

> *"I am the way, the truth, and the life. No one can come to the Father except through me."*
>
> – John 14:6 (NLT).

Jesus' story is represented by five symbols. The meanings of the symbols are:

He Came He Died He Arose He Ascended He's Coming Back

In the following chapters each of these symbols will be explained more fully using verses from the Bible. The Bible tells us what God wants us to know—and that includes what He wants us to know about how we can have a personal relationship with Him.

The Story of the Symbols

This book was written to explain how a series of five simple line drawings teach life-transforming truths. You may wonder where these symbols originated.

Over twenty years ago, Bill Smith drew these symbols on a chalkboard while speaking about the life of Jesus at White's Ferry Church of Christ in West Monroe, Louisiana. Mac and Mary Owen were in the class. They were impressed with the idea that these simple symbols could be used to tell the story of Jesus. Mac is a furniture builder and cabinetmaker. He began drawing the symbols on the back of items made in the shop of M&M Millworks. An employee of M&M, Keith Powell, burned the symbols into the bottom of a handturned wooden lamp.

One of these lamps was noticed by a customer in a local retail store. The customer admired the lamp but also became interested in seeing the company's other products. He called and asked to visit the shop. The Owens' son-in-law, Josh, answered the phone and invited the customer to visit the shop. Mac's response was that he was too busy so Josh would have to deal with the visitor.

Mac met the visitor on his arrival but busied himself with work. However, as Mac worked, he heard the man mention the symbols on the lamp. This caught Mac's attention so he listened closely and heard the man tell Josh, "The reason I came out here is I have to know what those symbols mean." Mac stopped what he was doing and joined the conversation which was about Jesus, not wood products. Mac selected a scrap of plywood from under the table saw. He drew the symbols on the plywood and explained the life of Jesus to the man. Within days, the man, whose name is Hal Dawkins, received the message about Jesus' life and ministry and asked Mac to baptize him. Hal says the reason he is a follower of Jesus is because someone took the time to draw a few symbols on a piece of wood. Today Mac doesn't need to draw symbols on scraps of wood because he has them tattooed on his left forearm!

THE STORY

He Came.

He Died.

He Arose.

He Ascended.

He's Coming Back.

He
Came.

He Came

God wanted to have a relationship with us so He sent His Son to lead us to Him.

> The Savior—yes, the Messiah, the Lord—has been born today in Bethlehem, the city of David!
>
> Luke 2:11 (NLT)

So the Word became human and made his home among us. He was full of unfailing love and faithfulness. And we have seen his glory, the glory of the Father's one and only Son.

– John 1:14 (NLT)

Biblical References

Matthew 1:18-2:23; Luke 1:26-56; 2:1-40; John 1:1-18

God created men and women to have a relationship with Him. The first man He created was named Adam and the first woman was named Eve. God gave them great freedom and a few restrictions to protect them. They had the ability to obey or disobey God's direction. They disobeyed. This attitude is called *sin.*

(The Creation story is found at Genesis chapters 1 and 2. Adam and Eve's sin is found at Genesis chapter 3.)

When Adam sinned, sin entered the world. Adam's sin brought death, so death spread to everyone, for everyone sinned.

– Romans 5:12 (NLT)

The word *sin* literally means *missing a target* or *taking a wrong road.* In the New Testament it refers to wrongdoing which violates God's law. (John 8:46; James 1:15; 1 John 1:8). Sin is a controlling influence in our lives. (Romans chapters 5—8, specifically, 5:12; 6:12, 14; 7:17, 20; 8:2). All of our sin is directed against God, though it may affect other persons. (Psalm 51:4; Romans 8:7). Sin offends and defies the character of God. It is expressed in the desire to be independent from God. Sin is rebellion against God because it is refusal to submit to His desire for our lives.

Adam's sin affected us. When he disregarded God's direction, his rebellion infected human nature. As his descendants, we were born with a fallen nature, a nature that will not always do what is right. Because God is perfect and sinless, people became separated from Him by their sin.

> *We were born with an evil nature, and we were under God's anger just like everyone else.*
>
> – Ephesians 2:3 (NLT)

> *For everyone has sinned; we all fall short of God's glorious standard.*
>
> – Romans 3:23 (NLT)

Despite their rebellion, God still desired a personal relationship, a deep connection, with people. Through Moses, He gave them guidelines to live by (called the law), which included the Ten Commandments. The law of Moses included the require-

ment of offering animal sacrifices by priests to remove the guilt of people's sin. However, these sacrifices did not result in the forgiveness of sins.

> *This is an illustration pointing to the present time. For the gifts and sacrifices that the priests offer are not able to cleanse the consciences of the people who bring them.*
> – Hebrews 9:9 (NLT)

> *The old system under the law of Moses was only a shadow, a dim preview of the good things to come, not the good things themselves. The sacrifices under that system were repeated again and again, year after year, but they were never able to provide perfect cleansing for those who came to worship. If they could have provided perfect cleansing, the sacrifices would have stopped, for the worshipers would have been purified once for all time, and their feelings of guilt would have disappeared.*
> *But instead, those sacrifices actually reminded them of their sins year after year. For it is not possible for the blood of bulls and goats to take away sins... Under the old covenant, the priest stands and ministers before the altar day after day, offering the same sacrifices again and again, which can never take away sins.*
> – Hebrews 10:1-4,11 (NLT)

God knew that we could not keep the law. To satisfy Him through our personal efforts, we would have to keep all of the rules and obey every regulation perfectly, completely. But people could not, and often would not, obey these laws; in fact, these rules caused us to behave worse. The rules condemned us. The law was not given to save us, but to reveal to us our weak-

nesses and remove our excuses. Our failure to obey teaches us that we cannot earn acceptance from God through our own efforts.

> *For the person who keeps all of the laws except one is as guilty as a person who has broken all of God's laws.*
> – James 2:10 (NLT)

> *When we were controlled by our old nature, sinful desires were at work within us, and the law aroused these evil desires that produced a harvest of sinful deeds, resulting in death.*
> – Romans 7:5 (NLT)

Holiness is God's innermost nature, which is separate and distinct from human nature. God's holiness refers to his moral perfection; but it also includes his power, eternity, and glory. His holiness evokes respect, amazement, and wonder in us.

> *Obviously, the law applies to those to whom it was given, for its purpose is to keep people from having excuses, and to show that the entire world is guilty before God. For no one can ever be made right with God by doing what the law commands. The law simply shows us how sinful we are.*
> – Romans 3:19-20 (NLT)
> See also Galatians 2:16 and 3:11.

Since we sin, we don't reach God's standard for acceptance of us because He is *holy.*

Our holy God will not accept unholy people. Our sinless God will not receive sinful people. Sinning against a holy, eternal God requires the death of the offender.

In fact, according to the law of Moses, nearly everything was purified with blood. For without the shedding of blood, there is no forgiveness.

– Hebrews 9:22 (NLT)

The word *Christ* is a Greek translation of a Hebrew word meaning *Messiah* or *Anointed One*. *Anointing* refers to setting someone apart for a special purpose or task. Kings, high priests, and prophets were anointed in the Old Testament. Jesus performed all of these roles (John 6:14; Hebrews 9:11; Revelation 19:16). Jews expected the Messiah to be a ruler like David who would deliver them from the occupying Roman army. But Jesus did not come as a military leader. He came to deliver us from oppression by sin. Jesus is referred to as Christ throughout the New Testament.

Rather than putting us to death for our offenses, God sent His Son to receive our punishment. Jesus came to be our substitute. He would receive the punishment that we were due. He would be the sacrifice for our sins.

That is why, when Christ came into the world, he said to God, "You did not want animal sacrifices or sin offerings. But you have given me a body to offer. You were not pleased with burnt offerings or other offerings for sin..." First, Christ said, "You did not want animal sacrifices or sin offerings or burnt offerings or other offerings for sin, nor were you pleased with them" (though they are required by the law of Moses). Then he said, "Look, I have come to do your will."... For God's will was for us to be made holy by the sacrifice of the body of Jesus Christ, once for all time.

– Hebrews 10:5-6, 8-10 (NLT)

God's Son was born to a fully human woman named Mary without the involvement of a man. She was made pregnant by the Holy Spirit. The child was named Jesus, which means *the Lord saves.* Jesus was completely human and fully divine at the same time.

> *This is how Jesus the Messiah was born. His mother, Mary, was engaged to be married to Joseph. But before the marriage took place, while she was still a virgin, she became pregnant through the power of the Holy Spirit... All of this occurred to fulfill the Lord's message through his prophet: "Look! The virgin will conceive a child! She will give birth to a son, and they will call him Immanuel, which means 'God is with us.' "*
>
> – Matthew 1:18,22-23 (NLT)

> *...Christ himself was an Israelite as far as his human nature is concerned. And he is God, the one who rules over everything and is worthy of eternal praise!..*
>
> – Romans 9:5 (NLT)

Jesus had to be completely human so He could die.

> *Because God's children are human beings—made of flesh and blood—the Son also became flesh and blood. For only as a human being could he die, and only by dying could he break the power of the devil, who had the power of death.*
>
> – Hebrews 2:14 (NLT)

> *But when the right time came, God sent his Son, born of a woman, subject to the law. God sent him to buy freedom for us who were slaves to the law, so that he could adopt us as his very own children.*
>
> – Galatians 4:4-5 (NLT)

Why Was the Time Right?

The coming of Christ was perfectly and precisely timed. *Politically*, Rome occupied Israel, which provided the region with good roads and peace. People could travel almost anywhere in the Roman Empire with relative ease and security. The apostles would later travel these roads carrying the Good News about Jesus. *Culturally*, more people than ever were becoming educated, so most people knew Greek or Latin. Even the common people understood Greek. The Greek of the common people would later be used to write the New Testament. *Spiritually*, the world was diverse but open, much like today. The worship of numerous gods by Greeks and Romans was being replaced by emperor worship and by rational, secular (non-religious) philosophies emphasizing wisdom. People were asking questions about the meaning and purpose of life.

Among the Jews, there was a renewed interest in the Bible, which was leading to revival on one hand (typified by the ministry of John the Baptist) and legalistic rule-keeping on the other (a strong Pharisaic movement). There was a strong desire for spirituality, though it was expressed in varied forms. The time was right for Jesus' arrival: relative peace, better roads, one widely understood language, and spiritual openness. God deliberately and specifically chose just the right time in history for Jesus' birth.

Since God is a spirit, people cannot see Him. Jesus was an exact replica of God's nature and character, but in human form.

> *Christ is the visible image of the invisible God. He existed before anything was created and is supreme over all creation.*
>
> – Colossians 1:15 (NLT)

> *"If you had really known me, you would know who my Father is. From now on, you do know him and have seen him!" Philip said, "Lord, show us the Father, and we will be satisfied." Jesus replied, "Have I been with you all this time, Philip, and yet you still don't know who I am? Anyone who has seen me has seen the Father! So why are you asking me to show him to you? Don't you believe that I am in the Father and the Father is in me? The words I speak are not my own, but my Father who lives in me does his work through me. Just believe that I am in the Father and the Father is in me. Or at least believe because of the work you have seen me do."*
>
> –John 14:7-11 (NLT)
>
> See also John 1:14 and Hebrews 1:3.

Jesus grew up just like any other person but He did not ignore or break God's law. He obeyed it completely. He satisfied fully all of the Old Testament's requirements and obligations. He lived an obedient, perfect, sinless life.

> *Jesus: "Don't misunderstand why I have come. I did not come to abolish the law of Moses or the writings of the prophets. No, I came to accomplish their purpose."*
>
> – Matthew 5:17 (NLT)

Jesus faced the same stresses, pressures, and temptations to sin as any other person. However, He did not sin. He lived a tempted, but sinless life so He could be punished in our place for our sins. If Jesus had done anything wrong, He could not have been punished for our sins. He would have been punished for His own.

> *This High Priest of ours understands our weaknesses, for he faced all of the same testings we do, yet he did not sin.*
>
> – Hebrews 4:15 (NLT)
>
> See also Hebrews 2:16-18; 7:26.

> *Christ suffered for our sins once for all time. He never sinned, but he died for sinners to bring you safely home to God...*
>
> – 1 Peter 3:18 (NLT)
>
> See also 1 Peter 2:22 and 1 John 3:5.

He
Died.

He Died

Our holy God cannot ignore our sins, so He sacrificed His Son's life on a cross for them.

> *He personally carried our sins in his body on the cross so that we can be dead to sin and live for what is right. By his wounds you are healed.*
>
> – 1 Peter 2:24 (NLT)

> So Pilate... ordered Jesus flogged with a leadtipped whip, then turned him over to the Roman soldiers to crucify him. ...And they brought Jesus to a place called Golgotha. They offered him wine drugged with myrrh, but he refused it. Then they nailed him to the cross.
>
> — Mark 15:15, 22-24 (NLT)

> *...It is not that we loved God, but that he loved us and sent his Son as a sacrifice to take away our sins.*
>
> – 1 John 4:10 (NLT)

Biblical References

Matthew 26-27:61; Mark 14-15; Luke 22-23; John 12-19

Jesus obeyed God completely but He did not do it in the way prescribed by the Jewish religious leaders. They accused Jesus of dishonoring God because He disregarded some of the rules they made. Jesus also spoke of God with too much familiarity, calling Himself God's Son. The religious leaders thought God should be honored, feared and respected, but not spoken of in a personal, relational way. People began to ask whether Jesus was the Messiah they expected to be sent from God to deliver them from oppression.

The religious leaders of Jerusalem—the priests and the teachers of the law—should have been eager to discover whether this extraordinary man was the long-awaited Messiah. Instead, they greeted Him with suspicion and hostility, seeing Him as an adversary and a competitor for the attention of the people. The religious leaders thought that they had God and His laws figured out. They reduced righteousness to a list of do's and don'ts which they instructed the Jewish people to obey. Then Jesus showed up claiming to be God's Son and working miracles. He even performed miracles on the Sabbath day in direct violation of their rules. Jesus' popularity continued to grow. He developed a following which threatened the authority of these religious leaders, so they plotted to have Him put to death.

The Sabbath, which was Saturday, the last day of the week, was designated as a day to rest from labor. The observance was begun by God who worked for six days creating the world and rested on the seventh. The day was blessed and made holy by God. It allowed people and animals to relax and be refreshed. The requirement is the part of the Ten Commandments.

Ten Commandments found at Exodus 20:8-11

> *Then the leading priests and Pharisees called the high council together to discuss the situation. ..."This man certainly performs many miraculous signs. If we leave him alone, the whole nation will follow him, and then the Roman army will come and destroy both our Temple and our nation."... So from that time on the Jewish leaders began to plot Jesus' death.*
>
> – John 11:47-48,53 (NLT)

Jesus not only performed unexplainable miracles, He also spoke of God in an intimate, personal way. He taught the Scriptures with authority even though He had not received the appropriate schooling and lacked the religious authorities' endorsement. The people were beginning to follow *Him* and seek *His* opinion about religious matters instead of *theirs.* This made the religious leaders angry! Jesus called them hypocrites for caring more about giving the appearance of righteousness rather than honestly seeking a right relationship with God. He criticized them for valuing knowledge of the law above application of it. These religious leaders were proud of their position, the respect they received, and the power they possessed over people as spiritual authorities and Scriptural experts—and Jesus threatened all of that! He was replacing them in the eyes of the people and ridiculing their authority, so they had to silence Him! That's why they had Jesus arrested in the Garden of Gethsemane and tried Him before the Jewish ruling council, the Sanhedrin. The Council condemned Him to death for calling Himself the Son of God.

Because Israel was under the jurisdiction of the Roman Empire, the Sanhedrin could not carry out a death sentence. The Jewish leaders took Jesus to Pontius Pilate, the Roman governor, in an attempt to have Jesus put to death. Pilate was appointed governor of the province of Judea by the Roman Emperor Tiberius. Pilate was charged with maintaining law and order in the region. He used violence and even murder to suppress threats of uprisings or riots. That's likely why the Jewish Council accused Jesus before Pilate of creating unrest, opposing payment of taxes to Caesar, and claiming to be a king. (Luke 23:2) These would be very disturbing charges to a man who was responsible for preserving peace in the province.

Pilate questioned Jesus and declared that he was not guilty of any crime. He knew that the religious leaders opposed Jesus out of envy. (Matthew 27:18) Pilate had Jesus whipped, hoping that would satisfy the Jewish crowd, but they wanted Him put to death. Looking for a way out, Pilate suggested that in keeping with a Passover custom, he release Jesus. The crowd shouted that instead they wanted Barabbas released, a criminal who had committed murder and insurrection against the government.

> *Now it was the governor's custom each year during the Passover celebration to release one prisoner—anyone the people requested.*
>
> *..."Would you like me to release to you this 'King of the Jews'?" Pilate asked. ...But at this point the leading priests stirred up the crowd to demand the release of Barabbas instead of Jesus.*
>
> – Mark 15:6,9,11 (NLT)

The Passover meal and the Festival (or Feast) of Unleavened Bread commemorated the Exodus of Israel out of slavery in Egypt. The LORD sent Moses to deliver the Israelites out of Egypt and into the Promised Land. Pharaoh (the Egyptian king) would not release the Israelites. God sent nine plagues of judgment, but Pharaoh still refused to let them go. The tenth plague caused the death of the firstborn son in every house that did not have the doorframes painted with blood. This protective blood had to be obtained from a sacrificed one-year-old sheep or goat without any defects. The death angel of the LORD *passed over* houses where blood marked the doorframes. (That's why the festival was named *Passover*.) Every firstborn son in Egypt was killed, including Pharaoh's own son. Pharaoh finally released the children of Israel. (Exodus chapter 12; Leviticus 23:4-5)

Jesus and His disciples were in Jerusalem for the Passover celebration when Jesus was arrested. At the Thursday evening Passover meal (called the *seder*), Jesus introduced the Lord's Supper. (Luke 22:7-16) After the meal, they sang a hymn (the *Hallel* from Psalm 116-118), then went to the Mount of Olives where Jesus was arrested. Jesus was crucified on Passover Day. The Passover pointed ahead to the Lamb of God whose blood would take away the sins of the world. (John 1:29) The Lord's Supper announces that this great work has been accomplished.

Pilate feared the Emperor. He had been in trouble with the Roman ruler for his mistreatment of the despised Jews. He was anxious about what these Jewish leaders would report about Him and concerned about how the Jewish people would react if he released Jesus. As a result, he gave in to their pressure and ordered Jesus crucified.

> *Then Pilate tried to release him, but the Jewish leaders told him, "If you release this man, you are not a friend of Caesar. Anyone who declares himself a king is a rebel against Caesar."*
>
> – John 19:12 (NLT)

> *Pilate responded, "Then what should I do with Jesus who is called the Messiah?"*
>
> *They shouted back, "Crucify him!"*
>
> *Why?" Pilate demanded. "What crime has he committed?"*
>
> *But the mob roared even louder, "Crucify him!"*

Pilate saw that he wasn't getting anywhere and that a riot was developing. So he sent for a bowl of water and washed his hands before the crowd, saying, "I am innocent of this man's blood. The responsibility is yours!"

And all the people yelled back, "We will take responsibility for his death—we and our children!"

So Pilate released Barabbas to them. He ordered Jesus flogged with a lead-tipped whip, then turned him over to the Roman soldiers to be crucified.

– Matthew 27:22-26 (NLT)

Crucifixion

Crucifixion was a cruel and painful form of execution. The word *excruciating* comes from the Latin word *excruciates,* which means *out of the cross.* Crucifixion was practiced by Romans to execute slaves, residents of regions controlled by Rome, and criminals convicted of serious offenses, but rarely Roman citizens. Romans were crucified only by order of the emperor for extreme offenses such as treason. For example, tradition says that Peter, like Jesus, was crucified, but Paul, who was a Roman citizen, was beheaded.

Crucifixion would occur outside of the city in a public place such as near a major road. The sight of a criminal humiliated and suffering on a cross would warn the people not to commit crimes. (Philippians 2:8; Hebrews 12:2) The Jews regarded anyone crucified as being under a curse. (Galatians 3:13) Jesus was crucified at a place outside of Jerusalem called Golgotha which means *Place of the Skull.* (Matthew 27:33; Mark 15:22: John 19:17) The name *Calvary* comes from *calvaria,* the Latin word for *skull.*

Jesus was likely crucified on a Latin cross which has an upright beam projecting above the shorter crossbeam. There are references in all four Gospels (Matthew 27:37; Mark 15:26; Luke 23:38; John 19:19—22) to the title, *The King of the Jews,* being nailed to the cross above Jesus' head. This title mocked the claim that Jesus was the Messiah. He was charged with encouraging rebellion against the Roman government. Before sentencing Jesus, Pilate ordered Him to be whipped. The whip was made of leather strips tipped with pieces of bone or metal that cut the skin, causing excessive bleeding and sometimes death. The Roman governor thought Jesus was innocent so He was likely trying to create sympathy among the Jewish people so he could release Jesus. (Luke 23:22; John 19:1)

Criminals sentenced to crucifixion were forced to carry the crossbeam from which they would be hung. A man named Simon was forced to carry Jesus' crossbeam. (Matthew 27:32; Mark 15:21; Luke 23:26) It may be that Jesus was physically unable to carry it due to weakness caused by bleeding resulting from his whipping. At the time of crucifixion, a victim was stripped, laid on the ground with the crossbeam under his shoulders, and his arms or hands tied or nailed to it. Jesus' hands were nailed to the crossbeam. (It may be that Jesus was nailed through the wrist or forearm since the Greek word translated *hand* could also be translated *wrist* or *arm* at Luke 24:39-40 and John 20:20,25,27.) The crossbeam was then lifted and secured. The victim's feet were tied or nailed to the upright post; Jesus feet were nailed. (Luke 24:39-40) The feet of a victim were attached clear of the ground, but not as high on the upright as is typically portrayed. The victim's body weight was usually supported by a peg on which the victim sat.

Death was caused by loss of blood, hunger, exposure, exhaustion, shock, suffocation or a combination of these conditions. Death was sometimes hastened by breaking a victim's legs. This would cause suffocation since the victim could not push himself up with his legs to breathe. The two thieves who were crucified on each side of Jesus had their legs broken (John 19:32), but Jesus did not because He was already dead. Pilate was surprised at how quickly Jesus had died. (Mark 15:44) A spear was thrust into Jesus' side to make sure of his death so that his body could be removed from the cross, as the Jews demanded, before the Sabbath began at sundown on Friday. (John 19:31-43)

Jesus endured agonizing physical pain on the cross, but His most severe suffering came from being separated from his Father when He took on our sin.

> *At noon, darkness fell across the whole land until three o'clock. At about three o'clock, Jesus called out with a loud voice, "Eli, Eli, lema sabachthani?" which means "My God, my God, why have you abandoned me?"*
>
> *Some of the bystanders misunderstood and thought he was calling for the prophet Elijah. One of them ran and filled a sponge with sour wine, holding it up to him on a reed stick so he could drink. But the rest said, "Wait! Let's see whether Elijah comes to save him."*
>
> *Then Jesus shouted out again, and he released his spirit. At that moment the curtain in the sanctuary of the Temple was torn in two, from top to bottom. The earth shook, rocks split apart, and tombs opened. The bodies of many godly men and women who had died were raised from the dead. They left the cemetery after Jesus'*

resurrection, went into the holy city of Jerusalem, and appeared to many people.

The Roman officer and the other soldiers at the crucifixion were terrified by the earthquake and all that had happened. They said, "This man truly was the Son of God!"

– Matthew 27:45-54 (NLT)

Even though Jesus was put to death by a Roman official under pressure from Jewish religious leaders and Jewish citizens, it was God who determined that his Son would die.

"Why don't you talk to me?" Pilate demanded. "Don't you realize that I have the power to release you or crucify you?"

Then Jesus said, "You would have no power over me at all unless it were given to you from above. So the one who handed me over to you has the greater sin."

– John 17:10-11 (NLT)

"...For Herod Antipas, Pontius Pilate the governor, the Gentiles, and the people of Israel were all united against Jesus, your holy servant, whom you anointed. But everything they did was determined beforehand according to your will.

– Acts 4:27-28 (NLT)

Then Peter stepped forward with the eleven other apostles and shouted to the crowd,... "People of Israel, listen! God publicly endorsed Jesus the Nazarene by doing powerful miracles, wonders, and signs through him, as you well know. But God knew what would happen, and his prearranged plan was carried out when Jesus was betrayed. With the help of lawless Gentiles, you nailed him to a cross and killed him.

– Acts 2:14,22-23 (NLT)

These Jews and Romans were all responsible for their evil deeds and yet, the betrayal, arrest, false accusation, wrongful conviction and undeserved death of Christ carried out God's purpose. God determined to provide forgiveness for their sins and ours. He decided to punish our sins by putting his Son to death. He did this because of his love for us.

> *"For God loved the world so much that he gave his one and only Son, so that everyone who believes in him will not perish but have eternal life."*
>
> – John 3:16 (NLT)

> *...It is not that we loved God, but that he loved us and sent his Son as a sacrifice to take away our sins.*
>
> – 1 John 4:10 (NLT)

Jesus was falsely accused and wrongfully convicted of the crime of blasphemy, an offense against God. Since He was innocent of any crime, and any sin, His punishment and death were undeserved, so they could be credited to us. He substituted Himself for us, taking the punishment and death which were due to us because of our sins. (Remember that God's law required sin to be punished by death). Jesus' death removed our separation from God. God could accept us and come into relationship with us without compromising His holiness or justice.

> *But those who depend on the law to make them right with God are under his curse, for the Scriptures say, "Cursed is everyone who does not observe and obey all the commands that are written in God's Book of the Law." ...But Christ has rescued us from the curse pronounced by the law. When he was hung on the cross, he took upon himself the curse for our wrongdoing. For it is written in the Scriptures, "Cursed is everyone who is hung on a tree."*
>
> – Galatians 3:10,13 (NLT)

He personally carried our sins in his body on the cross so that we can be dead to sin and live for what is right. By his wounds you are healed.

– 1 Peter 2:24 (NLT)

See also Matthew 20:28 and Hebrews 12:2.

Jesus willingly offered Himself over to death. His life was not taken from Him.

And even as Jesus said this, Judas, one of the twelve disciples, arrived with a crowd of men armed with swords and clubs. They had been sent by the leading priests and elders of the people. ...But one of the men with Jesus pulled out his sword and struck the high priest's slave, slashing off his ear.
"Put away your sword," Jesus told him. "Those who use the sword will die by the sword. Don't you realize that I could ask my Father for thousands of angels to protect us, and he would send them instantly? But if I did, how would the Scriptures be fulfilled that describe what must happen now?"

– Matthew 26:47,51-54 (NLT)

"The Father loves me because I sacrifice my life so I may take it back again. No one can take my life from me. I sacrifice it voluntarily. For I have the authority to lay it down when I want to and also to take it up again. For this is what my Father has commanded."

– John 10:17-18 (NLT)

See also Ephesians 5:2 and Philippians 2:6-8.

After his death, Jesus was buried in a tomb owned by one of his followers.

As evening approached, Joseph, a rich man from Arimathea who had become a follower of Jesus, went to Pilate and asked for Jesus' body. And Pilate issued an order to release it to him. Joseph took the body and wrapped it in a long sheet of clean linen cloth. He placed it in his own new tomb, which had been carved out of the rock. Then he rolled a great stone across the entrance and left. Both Mary Magdalene and the other Mary were sitting across from the tomb and watching.

– Matthew 27:57-61 (NLT)

In first century Judea, tombs were rectangular chambers cut into rock. Sometimes they were located in abandoned quarries. The tomb would have a small, low entrance which required a person to bend over to enter. (John 20:5) The tomb where Jesus was buried was blocked by a round stone (like a mill stone) which would be rolled in a slanted track into place in front of the opening. Some entrances were blocked with a stone which served as a plug that was dragged, pushed, or rolled into place. Blocking the entrance to the tomb prevented animals from entering to eat the corpse. (Matthew 27:60;28:2; Mark 15:46;16:3; Luke 24:2)

Jews did not practice cremation or embalming. They did not use coffins. Corpses were laid on benches or shelves cut into the walls of the cave. They were wrapped in linen cloth and left in the tombs until the body decomposed (usually one to three years). The bones would be collected and stored, with the larger bones on bottom, in a burial box called an ossuary. This practice allowed a tomb to be reused.

The next day, on the Sabbath, the leading priests and Pharisees went to see Pilate. They told him, "Sir, we remember what that deceiver once said while he was still alive: 'After three days I will rise from the dead.' So we request that you seal the tomb until the third day. This will prevent his disciples from coming and stealing his body and then telling everyone he was raised from the dead! If that happens, we'll be worse off than we were at first."

Pilate replied, "Take guards and secure it the best you can." So they sealed the tomb and posted guards to protect it.

– Matthew 27:62-66 (NLT)

He
Arose.

He Arose

After three days in a tomb, Jesus was raised from the dead, proving that God accepted His sacrifice for our sins.

> ...the angel said, "Don't be alarmed. You are looking for Jesus of Nazareth, who was crucified. He isn't here! He is risen from the dead! Look, this is where they laid his body.
>
> — Mark 16:6 (NLT)

And he was shown to be the Son of God when he was raised from the dead by the power of the Holy Spirit. He is Jesus Christ our Lord.

– Romans 1:4 (NLT)

He was handed over to die because of our sins, and he was raised to life to make us right with God.

– Romans 4:25 (NLT)

Biblical References

Matthew 28; Mark 16; Luke 24; John 20

After three days in the tomb, Jesus came back to life and left the grave.

Early on Sunday morning, as the new day was dawning, Mary Magdalene and the other Mary went out to visit the tomb.

Suddenly there was a great earthquake! For an angel of the Lord came down from heaven, rolled aside the stone, and sat on it. His face shone like lightning, and his clothing was as white as snow. The guards shook with fear when they saw him, and they fell into a dead faint.

Then the angel spoke to the women. "Don't be afraid!" he said. "I know you are looking for Jesus, who was crucified. He isn't here! He is risen from the dead, just as he said would happen. Come, see where his body was lying. And now, go quickly and tell his disciples that he has risen from the dead, and he is going ahead of you to Galilee. You will see him there. Remember what I have told you."

The women ran quickly from the tomb. They were very frightened but also filled with great joy, and they rushed to give the disciples the angel's message. And as they went, Jesus met them and greeted them. And they ran to him, grasped his feet, and worshiped him. Then Jesus said to them, "Don't be afraid! Go tell my brothers to leave for Galilee, and they will see me there."

– Matthew 28:1-10 (NLT)

Jesus' resurrection is essential to the Christian faith. It is referred to throughout the New Testament as a fact.

For if there is no resurrection of the dead, then Christ has not been raised either. And if Christ has not been raised, then all our preaching is useless, and your faith is useless. ...And if Christ has not been raised, then your faith is useless and you are still guilty of your sins. In that case, all who have died believing in Christ are lost! And if our hope in Christ is only for this life, we are more to be pitied than anyone in the world.

1 Corinthians 15:13-14,17-19 (NLT)

See also John 10:18; Acts 2:24;4:10;13:34-35;17:31; Romans 1:4; 8:11; Ephesians 1:19-20; Philippians 3:10; Colossians 2:12; 2 Timothy 2:8 and 1 Peter 1:3,21;3:18.

Jesus predicted His resurrection prior to his arrest.

> *"All right," Jesus replied. "Destroy this temple, and in three days I will raise it up."*
>
> *"What!" they exclaimed. "It has taken fortysix years to build this Temple, and you can rebuild it in three days?" But when Jesus said "this temple," he meant his own body. After he was raised from the dead, his disciples remembered he had said this, and they believed both the Scriptures and what Jesus had said.*
>
> – John 2:19-22 (NLT)
>
> Also, Luke 24:44-46.

Jesus remained on earth for forty days following his death to prove to his disciples that He really was alive and not a ghost. He even ate with them.

> *During the forty days after his crucifixion, he appeared to the apostles from time to time, and he proved to them in many ways that he was actually alive. And he talked to them about the Kingdom of God.*
>
> – Acts 1:3 (NLT)

> *"Why are you frightened?" he asked. "Why are your hearts filled with doubt? Look at my hands. Look at my feet. You can see that it's really me. Touch me and make sure that I am not a ghost, because ghosts don't have bodies, as you see that I do." As he spoke, he showed them his hands and his feet.*
>
> – Luke 24:38-40 (NLT)
>
> See also Jesus' discussion with "doubting" Thomas at John 20:24-29.

> *Still they stood there in disbelief, filled with joy and wonder. Then he asked them, "Do you have anything here to eat?" They gave him a piece of broiled fish, and he ate it as they watched.*
>
> – Luke 24:41-43 (NLT)

A dead person coming back to life is very difficult to believe. Our belief in the resurrection is based on faith, but not blind faith. There is evidence in the Bible that supports the fact that Jesus was raised from the dead.

Evidences for the Resurrection of Jesus

All four of the gospels—Matthew, Mark, Luke and John—tell the story of Jesus' resurrection, but how can we determine whether the story is true?

Evidence #1: The differences in the Gospel accounts.

The fact that the stories are not exactly the same is evidence that the story is true. If this story was merely a fictional tale, it would have been created by the writers of the gospels either separately or together. If the different versions of the resurrection were written entirely separate from one another, the facts would differ so widely that they would not even tell the same story, but they do! The four accounts cover the same occurrences involving the same people in the same locations at the same times.

The other option is that Matthew, Mark, Luke and John wrote a fraudulent story of a resurrection of Jesus together. If they had done that, the different versions found in the Bible *would not*

have had any differences. A conspiracy to defraud by the writers working together would have resulted in all of the versions of the story being identical in every detail, but we know that there are variations in the different versions.

Eyewitnesses of an event always describe the scene differently because their perspectives and what they deem most important are different. When eyewitnesses report exactly the same facts in *every* detail, it is evidence that they are working together or using a common script. These small differences in the biblical accounts of Jesus' resurrection are actually evidence for their truthfulness. They each reflect the viewpoint and interests of the writer.

Evidence #2: The disappearance of Jesus' body.

Jesus' body was missing from the tomb where He was placed after His death. The only possible explanations for the disappearance of the body were that Jesus' corpse was removed by someone or Jesus came back alive and left the tomb. If Jesus' dead body was removed, it had to be taken by either enemies or friends. Jesus' adversaries included the Jewish religious leaders and the Roman authorities. His allies included His disciples and followers.

Jesus' enemies might have removed his corpse to prevent His disciples from taking and hiding it, then claiming a miraculous resurrection to strengthen their following. But *they would have brought out the body* when the disciples started declaring that Jesus was raised from the dead. That would have destroyed the disciples' credibility and ended their movement. If Jesus' opponents did not display the body, it was because they did not have it. The Bible supports that position.

A meeting of all the religious leaders was called, and they decided to bribe the soldiers. They told the soldiers, "You must say, 'Jesus' disciples came during the night while we were sleeping, and they stole his body.'" ...So the guards accepted the bribe and said what they were told to say. Their story spread widely among the Jews, and they still tell it today.

– Matthew 28:12-13,15 (NLT)

The other alternative was that Jesus' disciples or followers removed His body. That is an unlikely explanation, because *his disciples wouldn't have died for a lie!* It's not likely they would have perpetrated a fraud which would result in their own punishment, imprisonment, and death. Historical writings supplemented by tradition tell us of the suffering Jesus' disciples endured for their beliefs: Matthew was killed by a sword; Thomas was run through with a spear; Jude was shot to death with arrows; Mark died after being dragged through the streets; Luke was hanged; Bartholomew had his skin stripped from him while he was alive; John was boiled in oil but escaped and was banished; James, the son of Zebedee, was beheaded; Barnabas and James, the son of Alpheus, were stoned; Peter and Andrew were crucified. Early church writings indicate that Peter was crucified with his head downward because he felt unworthy to die in the same manner as Jesus.

You might respond that people do sometimes suffer and even die for a lie, *but not when they know it is a lie!* The only reasonable explanation for the disappearance of Jesus' body was that He had been raised from the dead!

Evidence #3 – The number of eyewitnesses.

In the forty days following his resurrection, Jesus made ten distinct appearances to *more than five hundred different people,*

at different times and in different places. (1 Corinthians 15:5-8) He appeared in the garden near his tomb, in the room where His disciples gathered, on the road to Emmaus, and even far away in Galilee. Each appearance was characterized by different words and actions. He spoke, and ate, and let people touch Him. These people did not expect Jesus to be resurrected after his crucifixion. They misunderstood His claim that He would rise from the dead. Women went to the tomb on Sunday morning at dawn to put spices on a corpse—not to see a risen Savior! When they told the other disciples that He had risen from the dead, the disciples didn't believe them. Thomas said that he had to see it for himself—and he did! (John 20:24-29) There were so many witnesses that they couldn't have all been pressured to cooperate with a conspiracy to deceive. Paul, writing about twenty-five years after Jesus' resurrection, was so sure of the facts of the resurrection that he pointed out that most of the witnesses were still alive. The readers of Paul's letter could interview the witnesses for themselves. (1 Corinthians 15:6)

Evidence #4: The changes in the disciples' lives.

After Jesus' crucifixion, His followers were in hiding—afraid for their lives, bewildered, disappointed, disheartened. Peter, arguably the boldest of the disciples, had publicly denied he even knew Jesus for fear of punishment. (Matthew 26:69-75)

> *That evening, on the first day of the week, the disciples were meeting behind locked doors because they were afraid of the Jewish leaders. Suddenly, Jesus was standing there among them! ...As he spoke, he held out his hands for them to see, and he showed them his side. ...He ...said, "Peace be with you. As the Father has sent me, so I send you."*
>
> – John 20:19-21 (NLT)

After seeing Jesus alive and receiving the Holy Spirit to empower them, these disciples preached publicly, boldly, apparently unconcerned of what might happen to them. In fact, they were arrested and taken before the Jewish ruling council, but even this didn't frighten them. (This group included the persons who had orchestrated Jesus' crucifixion.)

> *The members of the council were amazed when they saw the boldness of Peter and John, for they could see that they were ordinary men with no special training in the Scriptures. They also recognized them as men who had been with Jesus. ...So they called the apostles back in and commanded them never again to speak or teach in the name of Jesus.*
>
> *But Peter and John replied, "Do you think God wants us to obey you rather than him? We cannot stop telling about everything we have seen and heard."*
>
> – Acts 4:13,18-20 (NLT)

Only an encounter with the risen Savior could explain this transformation of people who were disillusioned and afraid into bold and courageous preachers of the Good News of Jesus. The most convincing evidence of Jesus' resurrection *is the change in people* who have placed their faith and trust in Him!

The resurrection confirms the identity of Jesus of Nazareth as the divine Son of God, the Savior of the world, the long-awaited Messiah. Jesus was *fully* human, but had He been *merely* human—even an extremely wise and exceptionally spiritual human being—He would not have been raised from the dead.

And Jesus Christ our Lord was shown to be the Son of God when God powerfully raised him from the dead by means of the Holy Spirit.

– Romans 1:4 (NLT)
See also 1 Peter 1:21.

The resurrection reveals the relationship between God, the Father, and Jesus, His Son. It shows us who to rely on as our guide to reaching God. Many have claimed to be messengers from God but only one has received God's endorsement by being raised from the dead. Because Jesus was resurrected, we can know that a relationship with God can be secured through Him. Only Jesus can provide access to His Father.

Jesus told him, "I am the way, the truth, and the life. No one can come to the Father except through me.

– John 14:6 (NLT)

The resurrection of Jesus provides proof that our sins are forgiven. Jesus took on our sin—He became sin—and then bore the punishment due our sin. He died in our place as our substitute, received our punishment, and was raised from the dead to prove His innocence and provide our forgiveness. Without the resurrection, we would have wondered whether we had been forgiven. We would have spent our lives trying to earn forgiveness like followers of every faith lacking a risen Savior.

And if Christ has not been raised, then your faith is useless, and you are still under condemnation for your sins. ...But the fact is that Christ has been raised from the dead.

– 1 Corinthians 15:17,20 (NLT)

> *He was handed over to die because of our sins, and he was raised to life to make us right with God.*
>
> – Romans 4:25 (NLT)

Jesus' resurrection also provides assurance of our own resurrections.

> *I want to know Christ and experience the mighty power that raised him from the dead. I want to suffer with him, sharing in his death, so that one way or another I will experience the resurrection from the dead!*
>
> – Philippians 3:10-11 (NLT)

> *He will take our weak mortal bodies and change them into glorious bodies like his own, using the same power with which he will bring everything under his control.*
>
> – Philippians 3:21 (NLT)
>
> See also 1 Corinthians 15:48-49.

He Ascended.

He Ascended

Forty days after His resurrection, Jesus returned to heaven to prepare a place for us, to intercede on our behalf with His Father and to send the Holy Spirit to us.

When the Lord Jesus had finished talking with them, he was taken up into heaven and sat down in the place of honor at God's right hand.

— Mark 16:19 (NLT)

...I told you about everything Jesus began to do and teach until the day he ascended to heaven after giving his chosen apostles further instructions from the Holy Spirit.

– Acts 1:1-2 (NLT)

...he was taken up into a cloud while they were watching, and they could no longer see him.

– Acts 1:9 (NLT)

Biblical References

Mark 16:19; Luke 24:50-51; John 14:1-7, 15-31; Acts 1:6-11

Jesus remained on earth for forty days following His resurrection, teaching His disciples and proving He really had been raised from the dead. After this time, He returned to heaven. After talking with His disciples on the Mount of Olives in Jerusalem, He rose up into the air until hidden by a cloud. Jesus told His disciples that He would return to heaven so they would not think He had abandoned them. Several of them witnessed Him rising up into the air.

After saying this, he was taken up into a cloud while they were watching, and they could no longer see him. As they strained to see him rising into heaven, two white-robed men suddenly stood among them. "Men of Galilee," they said, "why are you standing here staring into heaven? Jesus has been taken from you into heaven, but someday he will return from heaven in the same way you saw him go!" Then the apostles returned to Jerusalem from the Mount of Olives, a distance of half a mile.

– Acts 1:9-12 (NLT)

Then Jesus led them to Bethany, and lifting his hands to heaven, he blessed them. While he was blessing them, he left them and was taken up to heaven. So they worshiped him and then returned to Jerusulem filled with great joy.

– Luke 24:50-52 (NLT)

See also Luke 9:51; John 6:62; 7:33; 14:28; 20:17; Ephesians 4:8-10.

Jesus returned to heaven to prepare a permanent place for each of us who have trusted in Him. He promised to return for us when everything is ready.

"Don't let your hearts be troubled. Trust in God, and trust also in me. There is more than enough room in my Father's home. If this were not so, would I have told you that I am going to prepare a place for you? When everything is ready, I will come and get you, so that you will always be with me where I am."

– John 14:1-3 (NLT)

In heaven, Jesus is *seated* in the place of honor and power at God's right hand. He is seated because He has completed the work necessary to obtain our forgiveness. The "right hand of God" is symbolic of having the authority to exercise the power of the King of the Universe. Jesus has power in heaven and also on earth. He watches over us, is aware of our needs, and speaks to His Father on our behalf.

For Christ did not enter into a holy place made with human hands, which was only a copy of the true one in heaven. He entered into heaven itself to appear now before God on our behalf. And he did not enter heaven to offer himself again and again, like the high priest here on earth who enters the Most Holy Place year after year with the blood of an animal. If that had been necessary, Christ would have had to die again and again, ever since the world began. But now, once for all time, he has appeared at the end of the age to remove sin by his own death as a sacrifice.

– Hebrews 9:24-26 (NLT)

I also pray that you will understand the incredible greatness of God's power for us... This is the same mighty power that raised Christ from the dead and seated him in the place of honor at God's right hand in the heavenly realms. Now he is far above any ruler or authority or power or leader or anything else—not only in this world but also in the world to come.

– Ephesians 1:19-21 (NLT)
See also Romans 8:34; Ephesians 4:8-10;
Hebrews 10:11-12 and 1 Peter 3:22.

Jesus' presence in heaven secures our salvation completely and permanently since He is the person who died for our sins. Anyone who approaches God through Jesus will gain access to Him.

Therefore he is able, once and forever, to save those who come to God through him. He lives forever to intercede with God on their behalf.

– Hebrews 7:25 (NLT)

Jesus warned his followers that He would return to heaven so they would not despair or think their faith was of no value after He left them. The disciples needed to learn not to rely on the physical presence of Jesus to encourage their faith. They needed to receive the Holy Spirit who would reside within them and strengthen them. The Holy Spirit would enable Jesus' followers to live as Christians. He would convict them of sin, convince them of truth, and conform them to Jesus' image (which is spiritual maturity). The Holy Spirit would equip and enable them (and us) to serve God on earth.

> *"But now I am going away to the One who sent me, and not one of you is asking where I am going. Instead, you grieve because of what I've told you. But in fact, it is best for you that I go away, because if I don't, the Advocate won't come. If I do go away, then I will send him to you. And when he comes, he will convict the world of its sin, and of God's righteousness, and of the coming judgment. The world's sin is that it refuses to believe in me. Righteousness is available because I go to the Father, and you will see me no more. Judgment will come because the ruler of this world has already been judged....*
>
> *"When the Spirit of truth comes, he will guide you into all truth. He will not speak on his own but will tell you what he has heard. He will tell you about the future. He will bring me glory by telling you whatever he receives from me. All that belongs to the Father is mine; this is why I said, 'The Spirit will tell you whatever he receives from me.'"*
>
> – John 16:5-11,13-15 (NLT)

"God raised Jesus from the dead, and we are all witnesses of this. Now he is exalted to the place of highest honor in heaven, at God's right hand. And the Father, as he had promised, gave him the Holy Spirit to pour out upon us, just as you see and hear today."

– Acts 2:32-33 (NLT)
See also Romans 8:11.

Jesus showed his love and concern for His disciples by asking God to protect them and to keep them united in their faith and love for one another. Jesus knew the danger and temptation they would face after He left them.

Now I am departing from the world; they are staying in this world, but I am coming to you. Holy Father, you have given me your name; now protect them by the power of your name so that they will be united just as we are.

– John 17:11 (NLT)

Jesus is in heaven today but He is spiritually present with us through the Holy Spirit.

Jesus: "For where two or three gather together as my followers, I am there among them."

– Matthew 18:20 (NLT)

He's Coming Back.

He's Coming Back

Jesus will return to the earth to defeat Satan, end evil, gather His followers and establish the kingdom of God.

"But when the Son of Man comes in his glory, and all the angels with him, then he will sit upon his glorious throne."

– Matthew 25:31 (NLT)

And then at last, the sign that the Son of Man is coming will appear in the heavens, and there will be deep mourning among all the peoples of the earth. And they will see the Son of Man coming on the clouds of heaven with power and great glory. And he will send out his angels with the mighty blast of a trumpet, and they will gather his chosen ones from all over the world—from the farthest ends of the earth and heaven.

– Matthew 24:30-31 (NLT)

Biblical References

Matthew 24-25; Luke 21; 1 Thessalonians 4:13-5:11; 2 Thessalonians 2:1-2; 2 Peter 3.

Jesus will return to earth from heaven. We call this His Second Coming, since His birth was His first coming. His return will mark the end of the earth as we know it. When Jesus returns, He will gather His followers and judge those who rejected Him. The return of Jesus is reported by many different writers throughout the New Testament.

And God will provide rest for you who are being persecuted and also for us when the Lord Jesus appears from heaven. He will come with his mighty angels, in flaming fire, bringingjudgment on those who don't know God

and on those who refuse to obey the Good News of our Lord Jesus. They will be punished with eternal destruction, forever separated from the Lord and from his glorious power. When he comes on that day, he will receive glory from his holy people—praise from all who believe. And this includes you, for you believed what we told you about him.

– 2 Thessalonians 1:7-10 (NLT)

...Now we live with great expectation, and we have a priceless inheritance—an inheritance that is kept in heaven for you, pure and undefiled, beyond the reach of change and decay. And through your faith, God is protecting you by his power until you receive this salvation, which is ready to be revealed on the last day for all to see...

So when your faith remains strong through many trials, it will bring you much praise and glory and honor on the day when Jesus Christ is revealed to the whole world... So think clearly and exercise self-control. Look forward to the gracious salvation that will come to you when Jesus Christ is revealed to the world.

– 1 Peter 1:3-5,7,13 (NLT)

See also Acts 1:11; 3:19-21; Romans 8:21; 1 Corinthians 1:7-8; 15:23; Philippians 1:6; Colossians 3:4; 1 Thessalonians 1:10; 3:13; 5:23; 2 Peter 1:16 and 1 John 2:28.

When Jesus returns, He will take His followers to the places in His Father's household that He has prepared for them.

"Don't let your hearts be troubled. Trust in God, and trust also in me. There is more than enough room in my Father's home. If this were not so, would I have told you that I

am going to prepare a place for you? When everything is ready, I will come and get you, so that you will always be with me where I am... Remember what I told you: I am going away, but I will come back to you again..."

– John 14:1-3,28 (NLT)

See also 1 Thessalonians 5:9-10.

When will this Second Coming occur?

Jesus spoke of signs of His Second Coming when He spoke to His disciples on the Mount of Olives. Some of the indicators of His return found at Matthew chapter 24:3-51 are:

- False Messiahs and prophets (verses 4-5,11,23-26)
- Wars and conflicts (verses 6-7)
- Natural disasters (verse 7)
- Persecution of Christians (verse 9)
- People turning away from faith and each other (verses 10 and 12)
- Increase in evil (verse 12)
- The Good News preached throughout the world (verse 14)
- The destruction of the Temple (verses 15-22)
  Note: This passage refers to the fall of Jerusalem in A.D. 70 and the desecration of the temple by the Roman emperor Antiochus Epiphanes. This ruler invaded Jerusalem and put to death eighty thousand men, women,

and children. He built an altar to Zeus over the altar of the burnt offering in the Jewish temple. He further defiled the temple by sacrificing a pig, an unclean animal under the Jewish law, on the altar. This event is the *abomination that causes desecration* (Daniel 11:31). He also stole the golden vessels and other sacred objects from the temple. He made the practice of the Jewish faith punishable by death. Jesus warned the inhabitants of Jerusalem to flee the city immediately when this invasion occurred. Some scholars also think that this event also forecasts the intense persecution that will occur in the tribulation prior to Jesus' return.

- The sun and moon will be darkened and stars will fall from the sky and the heavens will be shaken. (verse 29)
  Note: It is debated whether this is a literal description of events or a metaphorical, figurative reference to emphasize the catastrophic nature of events prior to Jesus' return.
- Indifference about Christ's return (verses 37-39)

– See also Mark 13 and Luke 17:22-37.

Despite mentioning many signs, Jesus did not tell his disciples when He would return; in fact, He stated that He did not know. He did say that everyone would be aware of His arrival.

> *"However, no one knows the day or hour when these things will happen, not even the angels in heaven or the Son himself. Only the Father knows."*
>
> – Mark 13:32 (NLT)

> *And then at last, the sign that the Son of Man is coming will appear in the heavens, and there will be deep mourning among all the peoples of the earth. And they will see the Son of Man coming on the clouds of heaven with power and great glory. And he will send out his angels with the mighty blast of a trumpet, and they will gather his chosen ones from all over the world—from the farthest ends of the earth and heaven.*
>
> – Matthew 24:30-31 (NLT)
>
> See also Revelation 1:7.

Jesus said that He would return in a surprising, unexpected way, like a thief who comes at night to burglarize a house.

> *For you know quite well that the day of the Lord's return will come unexpectedly, like a thief in the night. When people are saying, "Everything is peaceful and secure," then disaster will fall on them as suddenly as a pregnant woman's labor pains begin. And there will be no escape. But you aren't in the dark about these things, dear brothers and sisters, and you won't be surprised when the day of the Lord comes like a thief.*
>
> – 1 Thessalonians 5:2-4 (NLT)
>
> See also Matthew 24:42-44; 2 Peter 3:10; Revelation 3:3 and 16:15.

Jesus said that all of these events would take place while His listeners were still living. The apostles believed that He would return during their lifetimes. Jesus' statement meant that these terrible events would begin during their lifetime, not that He would return while His listeners were alive.

"In the same way, when you see all these things, you can know his return is very near, right at the door. I tell you the truth, this generation will not pass from the scene until all these things take place... However, no one knows the day or hour when these things will happen, not even the angels in heaven or the Son himself. Only the Father knows."

– Matthew 24:33-34,36 (NLT)

When Jesus returns, unbelievers will be judged and believers will be rewarded.

And just as each person is destined to die once and after that comes judgment, so also Christ died once for all time as a sacrifice to take away the sins of many people. He will come again, not to deal with our sins, but to bring salvation to all who are eagerly waiting for him.

– Hebrews 9:27-28 (NLT)

And now the prize awaits me—the crown of righteousness, which the Lord, the righteous Judge, will give me on the day of his return. And the prize is not just for me but for all who eagerly look forward to his appearing.

– 2 Timothy 4:8 (NLT)

See also Luke 12:38; 1 Corinthians 4:5; 1 Peter 5:4; 2 Peter 3:7; 1 John 4:17 and Jude 14-15.

When Jesus returns, He will raise deceased Christians from the dead and give all believers special bodies like His that can live forever.

But we are citizens of heaven, where the Lord Jesus Christ lives. And we are eagerly waiting for him to return as our Savior. He will take our weak mortal bodies and change them into glorious bodies like his own, using the same power with which he will bring everything under his control.

Philippians 3:20-21 (NLT)
See also 1 John 3:2 and 1 Thessalonians 4:13-14.

It will happen in a moment, in the blink of an eye, when the last trumpet is blown. For when the trumpet sounds, those who have died will be raised to live forever. And we who are living will also be transformed. For our dying bodies must be transformed into bodies that will never die; our mortal bodies must be transformed into immortal bodies.

– 1 Corinthians 15:52-53 (NLT)

Four Views of the End Times

There are four different views of of how Jesus' Second Coming will occur. They are referred to as *historic premillennialism, amillenialism, dispensational premillennialism* and *postmillenialism.*

All of these positions are held by people who respect the authority and reliability of the Bible. The differences result from the approach taken to interpreting Bible passages. The variations deal with the time and purpose of Christ's coming as well as the kind of kingdom He will establish. Although there are many distinctions between these positions, I will summarize only several of the major differences.

The primary points of divergence include the *millennium*, which refers to a thousand year reign of Jesus, and the relationship between the nation of Israel and the Christian church. Premillennialists (historical and dispensational) believe Christ will return and set up a kingdom on earth which will continue for one thousand years. Postmillennialists and amillennialists interpret the millennium as figurative, meaning an indefinite long period of time. Here is a brief summary for each view:

Historic Premillennialism

The millennium is a literal thousand years that will begin at a definite time in the future. The Second Coming will occur before the millennium begins. Prior to Jesus' return, the world will grow more and more evil. Christians, who make up the church, replace the nation of Israel as God's covenant people. (Romans 9:6-8; Galatians 6:16; James 1:1) Christians will remain on earth during a time of distress and suffering called the *great tribulation.* (Revelation 13:7) During this tribulation period, people who are not truly believers will leave the church which will strengthen and purify it. (Revelation 2:22-23)

Dispensational Premillennialism

The Second Coming occurs before the literal thousand year millennium begins at a definite time in the future. The world will increase in evil prior to Jesus' return. God will keep the covenant promises made to Israel. (Genesis 15:7-21) Israel and the church remain separate and distinct. Most dispensational premillennialists are pretribulationists who believe there will be a *rapture* (which means a removal) of all Christians by Jesus from the earth before the great tribulation begins. (Matthew 24:39-41; Luke 17:34-35; 1 Thessalonians 4:16-18; Revelation 4:1-2) Christians will escape the time of terrible suffering on

earth. (1 Thessalonians 5:9; Revelation 3:10) Some think the rapture will occur *during* the tribulation. They are referred to as mid-tribulationists.

Amillennialism

The millennium is a *symbolic* period, not a literal thousand years (2 Peter 3:8). The millennium represents the reign of Jesus Christ in the lives of Christians from the beginning of the church to the Second Coming. The great tribulation refers to troubles and persecutions throughout church history rather than to particular hardships at a specific time. (Revelation 13:7) Jesus defeats Satan through His death and resurrection which limits Satan's power on earth. (Revelation 20:1-3) Christians replace Israel as the people of God. (Romans 9:6-8; Galatians 6:16) References to "Israel" in Revelation apply to the Christian church. When Jesus returns, evil will be defeated and final judgment will occur. (John 5:28-29)

Postmillennialism

The Second Coming of Christ will occur after the millennial reign of Christ. (Revelation 20:1-6) The millennium is a lengthy time period, not a literal thousand years, when most of the world will hear and believe the Good News of Jesus. (Matthew 24:14; Mark 13:10) Jesus will not be physically present on earth. He will rule through the Holy Spirit. Satan will lose his power and influence over the world. (Revelation 19:19-20:3) A period of great tribulation may precede the millennium. The Second Coming, the resurrection of all people, and the final judgment will occur following the millennium. (John 5:28-29; Revelation 20:7-15)

Jesus' delay in returning allows more people to come to faith and receive salvation, so we must be patient.

Most importantly, I want to remind you that in the last days scoffers will come, mocking the truth and following their own desires. They will say, "What happened to the promise that Jesus is coming again?..."

But you must not forget this one thing, dear friends: A day is like a thousand years to the Lord, and a thousand years is like a day. The Lord isn't really being slow about his promise, as some people think. No, he is being patient for your sake. He does not want anyone to be destroyed, but wants everyone to repent.

– 2 Peter 3:3-4, 8-9 (NLT)

Dear brothers and sisters, be patient as you wait for the Lord's return. Consider the farmers who patiently wait for the rains in the fall and in the spring. They eagerly look for the valuable harvest to ripen. You, too, must be patient. Take courage, for the coming of the Lord is near.

– James 5:7-8 (NLT)

Jesus' return should encourage us toward faithful living.

And so, dear friends, while you are waiting for these things to happen, make every effort to be found living peaceful lives that are pure and blameless in his sight.

– 2 Peter 3:14 (NLT)

The end of the world is coming soon. Therefore, be earnest and disciplined in your prayers.

– 1 Peter 4:7 (NLT)

See also Philippians 4:5; 1 Timothy 6:14; 1 Thessalonians 5:10-11 and Titus 2:13.

At the Lord's Supper we remember the death of Jesus as we anticipate his return.

> *For every time you eat this bread and drink this cup, you are announcing the Lord's death until he comes again.*
> – 1 Corinthians 11:26 (NLT)

Jesus expressed urgency about his followers being prepared and keeping watch for His return.

> *"So you, too, must keep watch! For you don't know what day your Lord is coming... You also must be ready all the time, for the Son of Man will come when least expected."*
> – Matthew 24:42,44 (NLT)

> *He who is the faithful witness to all these things says, "Yes, I am coming soon!" Amen! Come, Lord Jesus!*
> – Revelation 22:20 (NLT)

See also Luke 12:36-40; 21:36; Mark 13:35-37; 1 Thessalonians 5:6; 1 Peter 4:7.

Accepting the Story.

↘ † ⌒ ↗ ↘

What if I accept what these symbols represent?

The symbols stand for significant events in Jesus' life. Accepting what the symbols represent means believing what the Bible says about Him. That's what faith is—believing that God forgives your sins because of Jesus' life and death. That is the way to receive salvation.

> *They replied, "Believe in the Lord Jesus and you will be saved, along with everyone in your household."*
>
> – Acts 16:31 (NLT)

Saved means forgiven of sins past, present and future; but also, freed from the domination and control of sin. You can no longer be condemned for wrongs you commit.

> *If you confess with your mouth that Jesus is Lord and believe in your heart that God raised him from the dead, you will be saved. For it is by believing in your heart that you are made right with God, and it is by confessing with your mouth that you are saved.*
>
> – Romans 10:9-10 (NLT)

> *So now there is no condemnation for those who belong to Christ Jesus. And because you belong to him, the power of the life-giving Spirit has freed you from the power of sin that leads to death.*
>
> – Romans 8:1-2 (NLT)
>
> See also John 3:18 and Romans 8:34.

When you do sin, you can admit your wrongs to God and He will forgive them so you can remain closely connected to Him.

If we claim we have no sin, we are only fooling ourselves and not living in the truth. But if we confess our sins to him, he is faithful and just to forgive us our sins and to cleanse us from all wickedness.

– 1 John 1:8-9 (NLT)

Being *saved* means that you have become a new creation and received a fresh start. Becoming a new creation is called being *born again*. You were born with a physical life, after being born again by the Holy Spirit, you have a spiritual life as well.

This means that anyone who belongs to Christ has become a new person. The old life is gone; a new life has begun!

– 2 Corinthians 5:17 (NLT)

Jesus replied, "I tell you the truth, unless you are born again, you cannot see the Kingdom of God... Humans can reproduce only human life, but the Holy Spirit gives birth to spiritual life."

– John 3:3,6 (NLT)
See also John 1:12-13.

When you are born again, you enter a relationship with God through Jesus. You are spiritually adopted into his family. When this happens, you receive the Holy Spirit to live within you permanently. The Holy Spirit confirms that you are God's child.

God decided in advance to adopt us into his own family by bringing us to himself through Jesus Christ. This is what he wanted to do, and it gave him great pleasure.

– Ephesians 1:5 (NLT)

...you received God's Spirit when he adopted you as his own children. Now we call him, "Abba, Father." For his Spirit joins with our spirit to affirm that we are God's children.

– Romans 8:15-16 (NLT)
See also Galatians 3:26 and 4:5-7.

When we become part of God's family, we can know that whatever happens in our lives can be used by God for our good and His glory.

And we know that God causes everything to work together for the good of those who love God and are called according to his purpose for them.

– Romans 8:28 (NLT)

The relationship with God that begins on earth when you trust in Jesus continues into heaven for all of eternity.

For you have been born again, but not to a life that will quickly end. Your new life will last forever because it comes from the eternal, living word of God.

– 1 Peter 1:23 (NLT)

For we know that when this earthly tent we live in is taken down (that is, when we die and leave this earthly body), we will have a house in heaven, an eternal body made for us by God himself and not by human hands.

– 2 Corinthians 5:1 (NLT)

Why would God do this for me?

The most well-known verse in the Bible says,

> *"For God loved the world so much that he gave his one and only Son, so that everyone who believes in him will not perish but have eternal life."*
>
> – John 3:16 (NLT)

God loves you. You matter to Him. He wants to have a close, personal, intimate relationship with you. He provided a way for you to enter this relationship. If you want to become a forgiven and accepted child of God, tell Him.

There is no perfect prayer, no essential words to bring about forgiveness and secure salvation. Just say a simple prayer in your own words. Admit you have sinned and ask God to forgive your sins because of the death of Jesus. Thank God for sending His Son to take your punishment. Ask God to grow you spiritually and help you learn to live and serve in the way He wants.

> ...*"Everyone who calls on the name of the Lord will be saved."*
>
> – Romans 10:13 (NLT)

Sources:

Wood, D.R.W.; Marshall, I. Howard: *New Bible Dictionary.* 3rd ed. Leicester, England; Downers Grove, IL.: Intervarsity Press, 1996, S. 1105

Strong, James: *The Exhaustive Concordance of the Bible.* Electronic ed. Ontario: Woodside Fellowship., 1996, S.G266

Vine, W.E.; Bruce, F.F.: *Vine's Expository Dictionary of Old and New Testament Words.* Old Tappan, NJ.: Revell, 1981; Published in electronic form by Logos Research Systems, 1996, S.O.

Mounce, William D.: *Mounce's Complete Expository Dictionary of Old and New Testament Words.* Grand Rapids, MI.: Zondervan, 2006, p.109.

Wiersbe, Warren W.: *The Bible Exposition/New Testament, volume 1.* Colorado Springs, CO.: Cook Communications Ministries, 2001

Barker, Kenneth L.; Kohlenberger, John R. III: *The Zondervan NIV Bible Commentary: Volume 2: New Testament.* Grand Rapids, MI.: Zondervan Publishing House, 1994

Arnold, Clinton E.: *Zondervan Illustrated Bible Backgrounds Commentary: Volumes 1 and 2.* Grand Rapids, MI: Zondervan, 2002

Bromiley, Geoffrey W.: *The International Standard Bible Encyclopedia: Volume 1: A-D.* Grand Rapids, MI: William B. Eerdmans Publishing Company, 1979

Arnold, Clinton E.: *Zondervan Illustrated Bible Backgrounds Commentary: Volume 1.* Grand Rapids, MI: Zondervan, 2002

Barker, Kenneth L.; Kohlenberger, John R. III: *The Zondervan NIV Bible Commentary: Volumes 1 and 2: New Testament.* Grand Rapids, MI.: Zondervan Publishing House, 1994

Rose Book of Bible Charts, Maps and Time Lines: Torrance, CA: Rose Publishing, Inc,, 2005

Boettner, Loraine: *The Millenium*: Phillipsburg, NJ: Presbyterian and Reformed Publishing Company, 1986

Clouse, Robert G.: *The Meaning of the Millenium*: Downers Grove, IL: InterVarsity Press, 1977

Note: If you would like to purchase the teaching DVD for this Study Giude, please contact the Brookwood Bookstore at 864.688.8300.

He Came.

Welcome to Session One of *The Story*. Many great stories have been told throughout history. Some stories have greatly inspired. Others have merely amused. But, only one story, *The Story,* changed time and eternity forever.

The story begins with "He Came," but that's really not the beginning of The Story. The Bible tells us very clearly that the events that occurred in a stable long ago were purposed from the foundation of the world (Ephesians 1:4). Christ's coming was not an afterthought. It was not an amendment to God's plan. Christ's coming was and is God's plan to reconcile human beings to Himself.

As you discuss a familiar passage of Scripture in this lesson, try to see it with new eyes. Do your best to put aside what you think this passage means (not that you were wrong), and take a fresh look at these words. You might even want to start this study with a new Bible translation or one that you don't typically use. We don't want you to miss anything. We want you to be open to anything new.

CONNECT 15 Minutes

For the sake of time, plan to address the *Group Guidelines and Agreement* in question two below; then choose either question one or three, as appropriate for your group. ***If your group has a limited amount of time, do your best to cover all of the questions marked with an asterisk (*) and allow the other questions as you have time.***

1. If your group is new or some people are joining your group for the first time, take a few minutes to briefly introduce yourselves.

2. *Open to the *Group Guidelines and Agreement* in the *Small Group Resources* section of this study guide, page 128. As you begin this first session take a few minutes to review the guidelines and make some decisions regarding your expectations for this study. A little time spent on this now can save a lot of confusion and disappointment over unmet expectations during the next few weeks.

3. What is the best gift you have ever been given? Why was it special to you?

45 Minutes GROW

HOST TIP: Always ask for volunteers to read, pray or participate in the discussion. Avoid calling on people. This tends to catch people off guard and unprepared.

Read: John 1:1-18

Watch the DVD.

DISCUSSION QUESTIONS

HOST TIP: If your group has eight or more people you may want to break into circles of three or four people for greater participation and deeper discussion. Then, come back together at the end of the discussion time and have someone report from each group the highlights of their discussion.

4. *The Gospel of John chapter one begins with descriptions of Jesus as the Word, the Creator, the Life-giver, and the Light-giver. What is significant to you about these descriptions of Jesus?

5. Verse 11 states that *"Even in his own land and among his own people, he was not accepted"* (NLT). Consider Matthew 2:1-6 and John 12:12-19 for some expectations about the coming Messiah and King. Why did Jesus' own people, the Jews, not recognize Him? How was Jesus different from what His people expected?

6. If Jesus was 30 years old today, what might He be like? What would the world think of Him? What would the church think of Him?

7. *Looking back over the history of how God revealed Himself to people, God used many different things: prophets, burning bushes, historic accounts, poetry and the Law. God desired to give an even better example, so He sent the Word (Jesus) as a person. John 1:14 says *"So the Word became human and lived here on earth among us"* (NLT). What might be lacking in our lives if the Word had not become human?

8. *Verse 14 continues *"He was full of unfailing love and faithfulness."* Why do you think this balance is important?

9. The religious leaders of Jesus' day had a strict, legalistic approach to following God. Jesus described them this way: "*...don't follow their example. For they don't practice what they teach. They crush people with unbearable religious demands and never lift a finger to ease the burden. Everything they do is for show...*" (Matthew 23:3-5). In contrast, Jesus told us "My purpose is to give life in all its fullness" (John 10:10).

How was Jesus different from the religious leaders of His day?

If you were around back then, what would the religious leaders' teaching have led you to think about God?

How did Jesus' coming change people's misconceptions about God?

What impression would Christians today give about God?

30 Minutes SERVE

Each session is built around one or two spiritual truths; but hearing the truth is not enough. We must act on it!

View The Video Segment "Telling Your Story."

10. *Verse 16 states *"From his abundance we have all received one gracious blessing after another"* (NLT) or literally "blessing upon blessing." One of the greatest gifts that we can give another person is the story of God's blessing in our own lives. Take five minutes to write out your "before and after" story of when Jesus came into your life. Take more time focusing on the changes than the details of your old life.

11. *Take two minutes to tell your story to one other member of your group. Then, ask them to tell you their story.

    (1) What my life was like ***before*** I met Christ.

    (2) How I realized I needed Christ.

    (3) How I committed my life to Christ.

    (4) The Difference God has made in my life since.

5 Minutes REACH

One habit that helps us grow spiritually is sharing with others what we are learning and what God has done in our lives. This section gives us an opportunity each week to identify people we can help come to know God's truths.

12. *In the *Circles of Life* diagram in the *Small Group Resources* section on page 137, write the names of people you know who need to know Christ or who could benefit from being part of a group like this one. Plan to call one or two of them this week and invite them to the Easter services at Brookwood, April 11-12, 2009. You might even plan an Easter brunch to spend some time with them before or after the service.

WORSHIP 15 Minutes

One way to worship God is to affirm your love and appreciation for him in prayer.

13. Share your prayer requests with your small group and record them on the *Small Group Prayer and Praise Report* on page 136 of this study guide. Keeping track of group prayer requests and answers to prayer would be a great role for someone in your group.

14. *Pair up in groups of two or three and pray for one another's needs, and for the understanding and wisdom to apply the lessons learned in this session.

Lesson 2

He Died.

He died. In a moment in time, all of history came to a conclusion. All of prophecy found a fulfillment. Jesus' death created a course correction for millions, if not ultimately billions, of souls destined for eternal judgment. One man, Jesus, carried the burden of sin and paid the ultimate price to give us life. *"For the sin of this one man, Adam, caused death to rule over many. But even greater is God's wonderful grace and his gift of righteousness, for all who receive it will live in triumph over sin and death through this one man, Jesus Christ"* (Romans 5:17). The only requirement that God places upon us is to receive the gift. While many of us would prefer to continue to carry the guilt and shame of our sinful deeds, God doesn't give that as an option. Grace provides a gift that we don't deserve and that's exactly why we need it so much. How great is the Father's love for us that we should be called the children of God!

Jesus' death is a remarkable intersection of time and eternity, pain and provision, prophecy and history, love, acceptance and forgiveness. This very real, historical moment is met with supernatural and miraculous occurrences. As you read the passage in this lesson and hear the video teaching, be careful not to get caught up in some spectacular "side effects" of Jesus' death. Rather focus on what His death means to your life and the lives of those around you.

CONNECT 5 Minutes

1. *If new members have joined your group today, have everyone introduce themselves briefly.

2. Tell the group about a time in your life when someone gave you something without expecting something in return. How did that make you feel?

GROW 35-40 Minutes

Read: Luke 23:32-49

Watch the video teaching now.

DISCUSSION QUESTIONS

HOST TIP: If your group has eight or more people you may want to break into circles of three or four people for greater participation and deeper discussion. Then, come back together at the end of the discussion time and have someone report from each group the highlights of their discussion.

3. *In verses 35-39, the soldiers, the crowd and the criminal say some pretty cruel things about Jesus. What do their criticisms say about what they thought Jesus could do?

4. Think about your own life and people around you: When did you think that Jesus should have done something, but He didn't? How have you dealt with that?

5. *How did Jesus respond to the criticisms at the cross? What is His attitude?

6. In verses 39-41, we read an exchange between the two criminals who were crucified with Jesus. What is different about their responses to Jesus?

7. Which of the two criminals was thinking about eternity? What was the other criminal thinking about?

8. *If you were hanging beside Jesus on the cross, which criminal would you be? Why?

9. *Verse 46 states that Jesus shouted "'*Father, I entrust my spirit into your hands!' And with those words he breathed his last.*" Jesus gave up His life. Technically, the Romans didn't kill Him. Jesus chose to die for us. What does Jesus giving up His life mean to you personally?

10. *How might your life be different without Jesus?

11. If anyone is absent from your group this week, ask someone to call or email them to let them know they were missed. It's very important for people to know they are cared about.

12. *In your life, where do you experience criticism or ridicule? Maybe you even face unbelief toward faith in Christ or outright mockery. What has your response been to these folks in the past? Looking at Jesus' responses to the mocking crowd, how can Jesus help you in these situations?

REACH 5 Minutes

13. *Last week you used the *Circles of Life* diagram on page 137 to write some names of people you know who need to know Christ or who could benefit from being part of a group like this one. How did your invitations go? If you haven't already done so, commit to calling one or two of them this week.

14. Perhaps you have family members who are not committed to Christ. Make a list of your family members and begin to pray for them this week.

10 Minutes WORSHIP

15. *As you finish your small group time, take time to share prayer requests and pray for the needs in the group. Record your prayer requests for the group on *Small Group Prayer and Praise Report* provided in the *Small Group Resources* section on page 136. Take time to report any praises from previous requests.

He Arose.

It's a quiet spring morning. Your friend has recently died. But, really he was much more than a friend. He was by far the most remarkable person you've ever met. He taught with authority. He healed the sick. He raised the dead. But, now he's dead, and part of you has died with him. You had hoped that he would lead the way out of oppression. Now despair creeps back in like never before. One last trip down the path to a tomb that holds the Hope of the world to remember what hope felt like. Soon, you will discover that a tomb cannot possibly contain that hope. Your world is turned upside down all over again. Hope is back.

CONNECT 10 Minutes

HOST TIP: If your group is unable to work through the entire curriculum, we have recommended one question or activity with an asterisk (*) in each section of the study.

1. If new people have joined your group, take time to introduce yourselves to each other.

2. *Looking back over last week, what took most of your time and energy?

3. Did you have any surprises last week? If so, what?

45 Minutes GROW

Read: Matthew 28:1-10 (this passage is read in the video, so find the chapter and follow along).

Watch the video.

4. If you were one of the Marys headed to Jesus' tomb, what would you have expected to find?

5. As one of Jesus' followers who left it all to follow Him, how would you have felt two days after His crucifixion?

6. If the angel had not been present at the tomb, what do you think the women would have thought happened to Jesus' body?

7. Imagine the sight of all of the Roman soldiers lying on the ground, the tomb is open and the angel is shining brightly. How would you have felt?

8. *Jesus' birth was proclaimed with great fanfare to the shepherds (Luke 2:8-14), yet in verse 7 the angel instructed the two Marys to go and tell the disciples. Why do you think there is such a low key approach to the news of the resurrection?

9. The text states that the women were "very frightened" and "filled with great joy" (verse 8). When have you ever felt that way?

In Ephesians 1:18-20 Paul prays for believers to experience wisdom and revelation *"having the eyes of your hearts enlightened, that you may know what is the hope to which he has called you, what are the riches of his glorious inheritance in the saints, and what is the immeasurable greatness of his power toward us who believe, according to the working of his great might that he worked in Christ when he raised him from the dead..."* (ESV).

10. *How is your daily life filled with hope because of Jesus' resurrection?

11. How would you look at things differently if you didn't have hope in Christ?

12. Ephesians 1:20 implies that God's power in each believer is the same as the power that raised Christ from the dead. What kind of power would it have taken to raise Jesus from the dead?

13. *If, indeed, that kind of power resides in you as a believer, how do you tap into it? What difference does that make in how you go about things? If you haven't established the habit of tapping into this power, what will it take for you to do that?

14. Today's teacher, Mike Hepola, spoke of our calling and inheritance in Ephesians 1:18-20. What did you learn about your calling and inheritance today that gives you hope for what lies ahead of you?

5 Minutes | SERVE

15. *Before next Sunday, call the folks you invited to church this past Sunday or just drop them a note. Find out how they liked it. Encourage them to come back, but don't pressure them.

5 Minutes | REACH

16. The miracle of Christ's resurrection defies logic. While there is plenty of evidence of Jesus' appearances after the resurrection, the best current evidence is what Jesus Christ is doing in your life. Take a moment and think about what Jesus has done in you recently: Prayers answered? Character improved? Attitude adjusted?

17. *This week pay attention to how the people around you respond to you. Observe how Christ is being revealed through you at work, at home, in your neighborhood, wherever you might go.

WORSHIP 10 Minutes

18. The fourth verse of the ancient hymn, *Be Thou My Vision** says:

Riches I heed not, nor man's empty praise,
Thou mine inheritance, now and always:
Thou and Thou only, first in my heart,
High King of heaven, my Treasure Thou art.

Ancient Irish hymn, possibly from the 8th Century, tr. by Mary E. Byrne

Considering that Jesus gave His all for us, how closely does your heart align with the words of this hymn? At this point in your life, what would you say is "first in your heart"?

19. If you have never invited Jesus to take control of your life, why not ask him in now? View the *How to Receive Christ* segment on the DVD or turn to page 123 of this study guide and discover how to receive this gift today.

20. *Maybe you don't feel a lot of hope today. What situations in your life are less than hopeful right now? Close your time together by praying for any needs expressed during your time together today. Record your prayer requests and praises on the *Prayer and Praise Report* on page 136.

He Ascended.

Jesus spent the 40 days following His resurrection with His disciples. That's enough time for His followers to start getting used to Him being around again. Forty days is also enough time to outlast any thoughts that Jesus might be some sort of hallucination, especially since He encountered so many of His followers during that time. He ate (Luke 24:42-43) but He also just appeared in a room with His disciples (Luke 24:36). Jesus' presence during those 40 days was more than enough proof that He did exactly what He said He would in rising up on the third day (Matthew 16:21). It also gave Him time to show His followers what awaited them on the other side of death. Maybe this is what helped them endure persecution and martyrdom. They already knew the secret: there is a life beyond this life that does not compare. But, ten days after Jesus ascended into Heaven, another promise was fulfilled: God sent His Holy Spirit to dwell in them. Suddenly, everything changed. Both the disciples and Jesus' followers today were empowered to do His work on this earth.

CONNECT 5 Minutes

1. *If Jesus appeared at your group meeting today, what would He think about your group?

GROW 35-40 Minutes

Read: Acts 1:6-11

Watch the Video.

2. Why were the disciples standing there staring into heaven? What would you have done?

3. *When the high priest asked Jesus if He claimed to be the Christ in Matthew 26:64, Jesus responded, "'*Yes, it is as you say.' Jesus replied. 'But I say to all of you: In the future you will see the Son of Man sitting at the right hand of the Mighty One and coming on the clouds of heaven.*'" Compare this with Mark 16:19, "*After the Lord Jesus had spoken to them, he was taken up into heaven and he sat at the right hand of God.*" What does it mean to you that Jesus is right next to God interceding for you?

4. *For many people Heaven seems so far in the future that it comes across as "pie in the sky." Jesus said that He was going to prepare a place for you (John 14:2-3). If our permanent, eternal home is in Heaven, how does that affect your perspective on daily life?

And I will ask the Father, and he will give you another Counselor to be with you forever—the Spirit of truth. The world cannot accept him, because it neither sees him nor knows him. But you know him, for he lives with you and will be in you. I will not leave you as orphans; I will come to you. John 14:16-18 (NIV)

5. What does it mean to you that God's Holy Spirit will always be present with you?

6. How do you experience the presence of the God's Spirit in your life? What helps you to recognize God's presence in you?

7. *Jesus said that He would "not leave you as orphans." Romans 8:14-16 tells us, *"For all who are led by the Spirit of God are children of God. So you should not be like cowering, fearful slaves. You should behave instead like God's very own children, adopted into his family—calling him 'Father, dear Father.' For His Holy Spirit speaks to us deep in our hearts and tells us that we are God's children."*

   According to these passages, what confirmation do we have that we belong to God?

8. *What does it mean to you that God speaks "deep in our hearts" by His Spirit? How have you experienced this?

SERVE 10 Minutes

9. *Take some time now to discuss what is next for your group. Will you be staying together for another study? What will your next study be? Turn to the *Small Group Agreement* on page 128 now and talk about any changes you would like to make in your group as you move forward as a group.

REACH 5 Minutes

10. *Someone said a long time ago, "There are no coincidences in a committed life." This week as you go about your routine, pay attention to what God is doing around you: who you bump into; an email or call from an old friend; an opportunity to help someone. These aren't accidents. Quickly consult God and then do what He says!

10 Minutes WORSHIP

11. Share your prayer requests and then break into pairs to pray for one another. Use your *Praise and Prayer Report* on page 136 in the *Small Group Resources* section to keep a record of answered prayers and remind you of the requests throughout the week.

He's Coming Back.

To many people the thought of Christ's return evokes images of elaborate dispensational charts and wild methods of calculating who exactly is the antichrist. While all of this might be interesting, it clearly misses the point of Christ's return. When Jesus was fixin' to ascend into Heaven, the disciples asked, *"Lord, are you at this time going to restore the kingdom to Israel?"* (Acts 1:6, NIV). Jesus quickly changed the conversation from Eschatology to Evangelism by answering, *"It is not for you to know the times or dates the Father has set by his own authority. But you will receive power when the Holy Spirit comes on you; and you will be my witnesses in Jerusalem, and in all Judea and Samaria, and to the ends of the earth"* (Acts 1:7-8)

As much as we might be fascinated by the "signs of the times," Jesus encourages us to be prepared for His coming and to spread the word to as many as possible. When times are tough and the pressure is on, the hope of Heaven is an awesome promise and telling your story is more important than ever.

CONNECT 10 Minutes

1. *If you knew that Jesus was coming back in the very near future, what would you do differently? ***(Caution: Please don't let your conversation drift into speculation or current events. Talk about how Jesus' soon return would impact your life.)***

GROW 40 Minutes

Read: 1 Corinthians 15:51-55

Watch the Video now.

2. *As you have heard, there are many views of when Christ might return. The reality is that no one can actually figure that out. What does it mean to you that Christ could return at any time?

3. What do you feel that you might be giving up when it is time to go to Heaven?

4. What do you feel that you will be gaining by going to Heaven?

5. This passage says that the "perishable will become imperishable" and the "mortal... immortal" (1 Corinthians 15:54). What is significant to you about that transformation?

6. *What are some things that seem so important now, but won't be important in Heaven?

7. What excites you about Christ's return?

8. *What concerns you about Christ's return? How can seeing the goodness of God and His love for us help you with your concerns?

SERVE 10 Minutes

9. *There are two things you can't do in Heaven: Share your faith with the lost and sin. While you have time here on earth, we encourage you to do more sharing. How can you demonstrate your faith to others this week? Is there someone who needs help? Is there someone you can pray for or even pray with them? Is there a relationship that needs mending? Name one person that you can "share" Christ with this week.

   Person's Name: ______________________________

5 Minutes REACH

10. *Are you ready for Christ's return? Do you belong to Him? From this lesson, we've discovered that Christ could return for all believers at any moment, but we also know that Christ could take any one of us at any time. If you have any questions about salvation, you might stay after the meeting tonight and view the video segment *How to Receive Christ* (or turn to page 123 in this study guide.) It's a five minute segment that explains what it means to make a decision for Christ and to be saved.

10 Minutes WORSHIP

11. Spend a few minutes now thanking God in prayer, taking turns to praise God for who He is in your lives and for the things He has done for you.

12. *Close your time together by pairing up and praying for one another.

How to Receive Christ

By Ned Gable

God loves you and he wants to be your friend.

He wants a relationship with you. This is sometimes so hard for us to accept. Think about this... where is the most amazing place you've ever been or would like to go? Would you want to be lying on the beach or driving through the mountains in the fall, skiing down a mountainside, or maybe just enjoying the flowers in your neighborhood park? How about your favorite animal? Do you still have a favorite animal or maybe you're too old for that. Think back for a second then, what animals amazed or intrigued you. One more, I know you can get this one... what's your favorite food? Ok, get all these things in your mind and let me ask you... who created these things. That's simple, God did. But why? He could have created one landscape, one season, one type of food but he didn't. He created an amazing world with such intense detail and variety that it captures and appeals to every individual in a different way. Why does God do this? Ask yourself, why do you give your children gifts to enjoy? Because you love them and you want to express that to them. This entire world is a giant expression of God's love for us.

God loves you and he wants a relationship with you, but there is a problem.

We have sinned. Romans 3:23 tells us that all of us have sinned and fallen short of God's standard. Romans 6:23 goes a step further and tells us that sin has consequences; it says what we have earned or deserve (the wages of sin) is death. Death... that sounds a little steep doesn't it? So I steal a cookie and I get the death penalty. That doesn't make a lot of sense does it? To understand this we need to understand the Biblical concept of death. Death is separation. Physical death is separation of body and spirit. We all have an eternal spirit but our bodies are temporary. Now, spiritual death is separation from God. Lost and separated from a God who loves us with no hope of saving ourselves.

Came to rescue us.

He died and rose again to pay the penalty that we owed for our sins. He died so that we wouldn't have to. Because of Jesus' sacrifice we no longer have to be separated from God. Remember Romans 6:23 says the wages of sin is death... but it goes on, the gift of God is eternal life in Christ Jesus our Lord. Jesus' sacrifice makes forgiveness for our sins and a right relationship with God possible and He offers it to each of us as a gift.

Now there's something interesting about gifts. If I offer you this gift, do you have it just because I offer it? No, you have to take the gift, you have to receive it. The same is true with God's gift. We didn't earn it. We don't deserve it. There's nothing we can do in and of ourselves to get it. But God offers the gift because He chooses to and our role is simply to receive what He has offered.

How does that happen?

First, we admit that we have sinned and repent of those sins.

Repent basically means "to turn away from." We're never going to be perfect in this life but to repent means that we don't justify or rationalize our sin, we recognize it for what it is and turn away from it.

Second, we must believe in Jesus.

John 1:12 tells us, *"to all those who received him, to those who believed in His name, he gave the right to become children of God."* Belief in Jesus has nothing to do with knowledge or mental assent. It is a transfer of trust.

Finally, we confess that Jesus is Lord.

Romans 10:9 says, *"if you confess with your mouth that Jesus is Lord and believe in your heart that God raised him from the dead you will be saved."* If Jesus is the Lord of my life, then I set Him and my relationship with Him as the center of my life. I stop living for my goals and my desires and I start living for Him.

Admit – Believe – Confess.

When this happens in our life we are changed. We literally become a new person. All of our sins and shortcomings are forgiven and ***we're adopted into God's family.*** We are no longer separated from God. We have a new relationship, a friendship, with Him that cannot be broken. What's more, we are given eternal life and that friendship will never end.

Small Group Resources

Group Guidelines and Agreement

It's a good idea for every group to put words to their shared values, expectations, and commitments. Such guidelines will help you avoid unspoken agendas and unmet expectations. We recommend you discuss your guidelines in order to lay the foundation for a healthy group experience. Feel free to modify anything that does not work for your group.

If the idea of a written agreement is unfamiliar to your group, we encourage you to give it a try.

We Agree To The Following Values

Clear Purpose

Grow healthy spiritual lives by building a healthy small group community.

Group Attendance

Give priority to the group meeting (call if I am absent or late).

Safe Environment

Help create a safe place where people can be heard and feel loved (no quick answers, snap judgments, or simple fixes).

Be Confidential

Keep anything that is shared strictly confidential and within the group.

Conflict Resolution

To avoid gossip and to immediately resolve any concerns by following the principles of Matthew 18:15-17 which begins with going directly to the person with whom you have an issue.

Limit our Freedom

To limit our freedom by not serving or consuming alcohol during Brookwood small group meetings or events so as to avoid causing a weaker brother or sister to stumble (1 Corinthians 8:1-13, Romans 14:19-21).

Spiritual Health

Give group members permission to help me live a healthy, balanced spiritual life that is pleasing to God.

Welcome Newcomers

Invite our friends who might benefit from this study and warmly welcome newcomers.

Building Relationships

Get to know the other members of the group and pray for them regularly.

Other

____

____

We Agree To The Following Items

- Childcare ______________________
- Starting Time ______________________
- Ending Time ______________________

If you haven't already done so, take a few minutes to fill out the Small Group Calendar on page 130.

Small Group Calendar

Healthy groups share responsibilities and group ownership. It might take some time for this to develop. Shared ownership ensures no one person has total responsibility for the group. Use the calendar to keep track of social events, mission projects, birthdays, or days off. Complete this calendar at your first or second session. Planning ahead will increase attendance and shared ownership.

Date	Lesson	Location	Facilitator	Snack/Meal

Frequently Asked Questions

I'd like to host a Small Group, but should I wait until I have more experience?

If you have a willing heart, a DVD player, and a few open seats in your living room, you can be a host. The DVD "teaches" the group. Before your group starts, you'll receive host training that helps you get the most from the DVD curriculum and gives you answers to your questions.

When will my Small Group meet?

Your group is welcome to meet on whatever day and time are convenient to your group. If you are doing this with the *The Story* series, then your group will start the week of March 29, 2009 and will end the week of April 26, 2009. Of course, there's always a little "wiggle room" if your group hasn't completed the study by then. If you are using this study after the original series, we would encourage you to view the Sunday message series along with this study.

What happens to my Small Group after our five weeks together?

Your group's members commit only for five weeks, but as you reach the end of that time, our hope is that they will want to stay together as a group. You may or may not choose to continue. If you decide not to, we ask that you help identify a leader among the people who want to stay. Training and support will be provided for these new leaders.

Who do I invite to my Small Group?

We suggest three primary sources:

- **Neighbors who go to Brookwood.** Consider having a summer cookout with them. Some of these neighbors may be eager to join your group. If you would like a list of people who live in your zip code, contact Lora Catoe at lora.catoe@brookwoodchurch.org.
- **People you know**–your friends and neighbors. Ask them to join you and encourage them to invite someone they know. They don't need to come to Brookwood or any church to take part in your group.
- **The Brookwood Church Website.** Please make sure that we have your accurate group information to include on the website. Prospective members will contact you via email.

I'd like to do the Bible study, but I'm not comfortable meeting with a group of strangers?

That's an easy one: do the study with people you already know. Simply invite your friends to join you for the 5-week study. Just attend one of the host orientations or contact Lora Catoe. You will be given the option to host an "invitation only" group. This way you can skip the signups if you would prefer to not do the study with new people. You will receive the same help and support as the other hosts.

Top Ten Ideas For Hosts

As you prepare to lead, whether it is one session or an entire series, here are a few thoughts to keep in mind. We encourage you to read these and review them with each new discussion leader before he or she leads.

1. **Remember you are not alone.** God knows everything about you, and He knew you would be asked to lead your group. Even though you may not feel ready to lead, this is common for all good leaders. God promises, *"I will never leave you; I will never abandon you"* (Hebrews 13:5 TEV). Whether you are leading for one evening, several sessions, or a lifetime, you will be blessed as you serve.

2. **Don't try to do it alone.** Pray right now for God to help you build a healthy leadership team. If you can enlist a co-leader to help you lead the group, you will find your experience much richer. This is your chance to involve as many people as you can in building a healthy group. All you have to do is ask people to help and you'll be surprised at the response.

3. **Just be yourself.** God wants to use your unique gifts and temperament. Don't try to do things exactly like another leader; do them in a way that fits you. Admit when you don't have an answer and apologize when you make a mistake. Your group will love you for it and you'll sleep better at night.

4. **Prepare for your meeting ahead of time.** Review the session and write down your responses to each question. Pay special attention to exercises that ask group members

to do something other than engage in discussion. These exercises will help your group live what the Bible teaches, not just talk about it. Be sure you understand how an exercise works. If the exercise employs one of the items in the *Small Group Resources* section (such as the *Group Guidelines and Agreement*), be sure to look over that item so you'll know how it works.

5. **Pray for your group members by name.** Before you begin your session, take a few moments and pray for each member by name. You may want to review the prayer list at least once a week. Ask God to use your time together to touch the heart of every person uniquely. Expect God to lead you to whomever He wants you to encourage or challenge in a special way. If you listen, God will surely lead.

6. **When you ask a question, be patient.** Someone will eventually respond. Sometimes people need a moment or two of silence to think about the question. If silence doesn't bother you, it won't bother anyone else. After someone responds, affirm the response with a simple "thanks" or "great answer." Then ask, "How about somebody else?" or "Would someone who hasn't shared like to add anything?" Be sensitive to new people or reluctant members who aren't ready to say, pray, or do anything. If you give them a safe setting, they will blossom over time.

7. **Provide transitions between questions.** Ask if anyone would like to read the paragraph or Bible passage. Don't call on anyone, but ask for a volunteer, and then be patient until someone begins. Be sure to thank the person who reads aloud.

8. **Break into small groups occasionally.** The *Grow and Worship* sections provide good opportunities to break into smaller circles. With a greater opportunity to talk in a small circle, people will connect more with the study, apply more quickly what they're learning, and ultimately get more out of it. A small circle also encourages a quiet person to participate and tends to minimize the effects of a more vocal or dominant member. Small circles are also helpful during prayer time. People who are unaccustomed to praying aloud will feel more comfortable trying it with just two or three others. Also, prayer requests won't take as much time, so circles will have more time to actually pray. When you gather back with the whole group, you can have one person from each circle briefly update everyone on the prayer requests. People are more willing to pray in small circles if they know the whole group will hear all the prayer requests.

9. **Rotate hosts occasionally.** You may be perfectly capable of hosting each time, but you will help others grow in their faith and gifts if you give them opportunities to host.

10. **One final challenge (for new or first-time hosts):** Before your first opportunity to host, look up each of the five passages listed below. Read each one as a devotional exercise to help prepare you with a shepherd's heart. Trust us on this one. If you do this, you will be more than ready for your first meeting.

    - Matthew 9:35-38
    - 1 Peter 5:2-4
    - Philippians 2:1-5
    - Hebrews 10:23-25
    - 1 Thessalonians 2:7, 8, 11

Small Group Prayer and Praise Report

Date	Person	Prayer	Praise

Circles Of Life

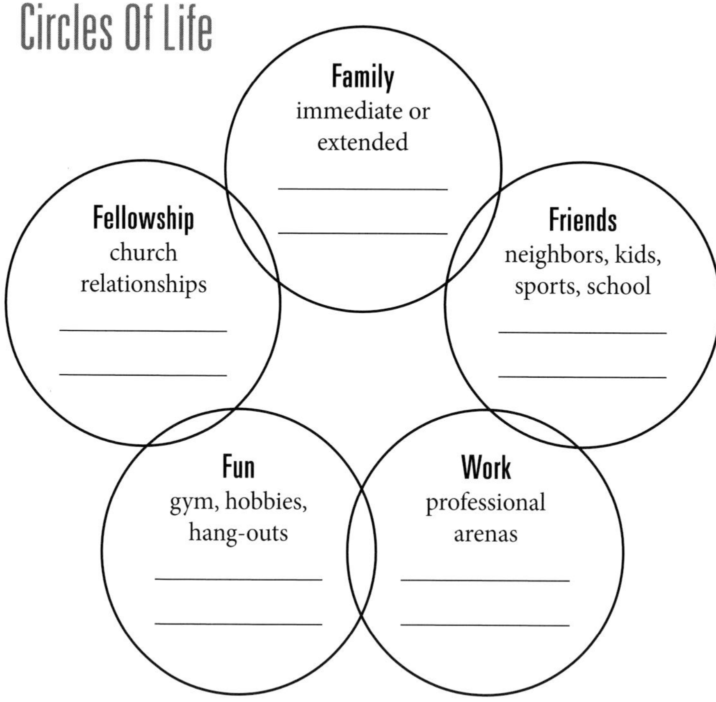

Follow This Simple Four-Step Process:

1. Prayerfully list 1 or 2 people in each circle.
2. Prepare the group for them. Share a few names with your group and update your progress.
3. Place a call to them.
4. Pick them up and bring them to your next meeting.

"Follow me and I will make you fishers of men."

– Matthew 4:19

My Small Group Roster

Name	Phone	Email

Author Bios

Perry Duggar is Senior Pastor of Brookwood Church in Simpsonville, South Carolina, which he planted in 1993. He has been happily married for over twenty years to Leigh Ann and has two delightful teen-aged daughters, Evan and Aubrey.

He grew up in a Baptist church and was graduated from a Catholic high school in Augusta, Georgia. Perry practiced law in Georgia before moving into a church vocation as a layperson. After two years serving in church ministry to confirm God's calling to pastoral ministry, he attended Reformed Theological Seminary and was graduated from Southeastern Baptist Theological Seminary. He thinks that these varied personal, professional and theological influences served to enrich his understanding of God and faith.

Allen White is the Adult Discipleship Pastor at Brookwood Church. In his 27 years of ministry experience, he has served as the Executive Director of Lifetogether.com, a small groups publishing and training ministry; as an instructor at the Global Bible Institute in Modesto, CA and as an associate pastor for 15 years in Northern California. Allen holds both a B.A. in Biblical Studies and World Missions as well as a Master of Divinity in Christian Education. Allen and his wife, Tiffany live in Simpsonville, South Carolina with their three children.